Little Ones Parents Teaching Guide

PROTECTING YOUR CHILDREN FROM SEXUAL ASSAULT

BY WILLIAM KATZ

With Illustrations by Mary Albury-Noyes

W9-BVS-350

Little Ones †

LITTLE ONES BOOKS
Young America, Minnesota, U.S.A.
and Toronto, Ontario, Canada

ISBN 0-920195-01-6

Little Ones Parents Teaching Guide

1st Edition Copyright © 1983, William Katz

2nd Edition Copyright © 1984 William Katz

Published by Little Ones Books
Young America, Minnesota, U.S.A.
and
Toronto, Ontario, Canada

Printed in Canada
Harmony Printing Limited
123 Eastside Drive, Toronto, Ontario M8Z 5S5

Introduction

Congratulations! You are about to begin an exciting and rewarding personal Bible study which will prepare you to lead one or more children through the Little Ones course entitled, "Protecting your children from sexual assault."

As a Little Ones teacher you will be asked, first, to complete this teacher's guide and to familiarize yourself with certain specific Bible verses, and the easy to follow, step by step children's workbook which accompanies the teaching guide.

It is very important that, no matter how well versed you may be in the scriptures, you *personally* complete the teacher's guide *before* you proceed with the children's workbook.

By carefully following these guidelines you will be a more effective teacher and you will personally grow in your knowledge and understanding of the important message contained in the Word of God relating to our children.

Again, congratulations on your commitment to help protect His little ones and may God bless you in this effort.

The Little Ones Teaching Kit

This Little Ones teaching kit is intended to help you effectively communicate, to children, the reality of sexual assault. It is a Bible oriented, family supported study which depends upon an understanding of the Holy Scriptures and will only be effective if you and your child work on the course material together.

Depending upon your personal knowledge of the Bible, the teacher's preparation for this course will require approximately two to three hours of reading and study. The children's workbook can then be taught in approximately eight sessions of from 30 to 60 minutes each.

The teaching may be at any reasonable interval but we recommend that sessions be given not more frequently than one each day and not less frequently than once a week.

The best teaching interval is one that allows the child to retain as much information as possible, while at the same time, allowing him or her to formulate and to ask questions between the periods of study and instruction.

Try to be sensitive to the needs and individual capabilities of each and every child. Don't rush and always try to allow the child to move at his or her own pace.

Remember, like all Bible study, this course is a growing experience. Take the time to reflect, enjoy and share God's wonderful message and His protecting knowledge with your child.

It really will be something that you'll both remember for the rest of your lives.

Notes

The Little Ones Philosophy

"The Obedient Christian Child Is God's Gift To Us, At Risk In The World"

God certainly blesses the believing Christian family in many ways, but no blessing, within any family, can be compared with God's gift of a child into the union of husband and wife.

The birth of a child and that child's life on earth are part of the moral and spiritual contract between the Christian parent and God.

Unquestionably, children are gifts from God;

> *And he lifted up his eyes, and saw the women and the children: and said, Who are those with thee?*
>
> *And he said, The children which God hath graciously given thy servant. (Genesis 33:5) (KJV)*
>
> *And Israel beheld Joseph's sons, and said, Who are these?*
>
> *And Joseph said unto his father, They are my sons, whom God hath given me in this place. And he said, Bring them, I pray thee, unto me, and I will bless them. (Genesis 48:8,9) (KJV)*
>
> *Lo, children are a heritage of the Lord: and the fruit of the womb is his reward.*

As arrows are in the hand of a mighty man; so are children of one's youth.

Happy is the man that hath his quiver full of them: they shall not be ashamed, but they shall speak with the enemies in the gate. (Psalm 127:3-5) (KJV)

Their care, nourishment, training and well being are directed by God's Word;

But Hannah went not up; for she said unto her husband, I will not go up until the child be weaned, and then I will bring him, that he may appear before the Lord, and there abide for ever. (I Samuel 1:22) (KJV)

And, ye fathers, provoke not your children to wrath: but bring them up in the nurture and admonition of the Lord. (Ephesians 6:4) (KJV)

Train up a child in the way he should go: and when he is old, he will not depart from it. (Proverbs 22:6) (KJV)

And thou shalt teach them diligently unto thy children, and shalt talk of them when thou sittest in thine house, and when thou walkest by the way and when thou liest down, and when thou risest up. (Deuteronomy 6:7) (KJV)

God's law also requires much of the Christian child in his relationship with his parents;

Children, obey your parents in the Lord: for this is right. (Ephesians 6:1) (KJV)

Furthermore we have had fathers of our flesh which corrected us, and we gave them reverence: shall we not much rather be in subjection unto the Father of spirits and live? (Hebrews 12:9) (KJV)

But the Bible also teaches us that Satan would undo God's work and that Satan will misuse God's Word:

Then was Jesus led up of the Spirit into the wilderness to be tempted of the devil.

And when he had fasted forty days and forty nights, he was afterward hungered.

And when the tempter came to him, he said, If thou be the Son of God, command that these stones be made of bread.

But he answered and said, It is written, Man shall not live by bread alone, but by every word that proceedeth out of the mouth of God.

Then the devil taketh him up into the holy city, and setteth him on a pinnacle of the temple, And saith unto him, If thou be the Son of God, cast thyself down: for it is written, of God, cast thyself down: for it is written, He shall give his angels charge concerning thee: and in their hands they shall bear thee up, lest at any time thou dash thy foot against a stone. (St. Matthew 4:1-6) (KJV)

Furthermore, Satan places great significance upon and always strives for the destruction of any person who is truly a servant of the Lord.

Again there was a day when the sons of God came to present themselves before the Lord and Satan came also among them to present himself before the Lord.

And the Lord said unto Satan, From whence comest thou? And Satan answered the Lord, and said, From going to and fro in the earth, and from walking up and down in it.

And the Lord said unto Satan, Hast thou considered my servant Job, that there is none like him in the earth, a perfect and upright man, one that feareth God, and escheweth evil? and still he holdeth fast his integrity, although thou movedst me against him, to destroy him without cause.

And Satan answered the Lord, and said, Skin for skin, yea, all that a man hath will he give for his life.

But put forth thine hand now, and touch his bone and his flesh, and he will curse thee to thy face. And the Lord said unto Satan, Behold, he is in thine hand: but save his life.

So went Satan forth from the presence of the Lord, and smote Job with sore boils from the sole of his foot unto his crown. (Job 2:1-7) (KJV)

> *Be sober, be vigilant; because your adversary the devil,*
> *as a roaring lion, walketh about, seeking whom he may*
> *devour: (I Peter 5:8) (KJV)*

We also see in the 18th chapter of the Gospel according to St. Matthew that children are to be particularly protected from evil;

> *But whoso shall offend one of these little ones which be-*
> *lieve in me, it were better for him that a millstone were*
> *hanged about his neck, and that he were drowned in the*
> *depth of the sea. (St. Matthew 18:6) (KJV)*

and in the 9th chapter of the Gospel according to St. Luke we are taught that things which effect children touch God, Himself.

> *And said unto them, Whosoever shall receive this child*
> *in my name receiveth me: and whosoever shall receive*
> *me receiveth him that sent me: for he that is least*
> *among you all, the same shall be great. (Luke 9:48)*
> *(KJV)*

Keeping all this in mind, it is important for you as a Christian parent and as a teacher of this course to understand the very real and immediate danger that is created by the conflict between the godly values we teach our children and Satan's attempted misuse of those values to achieve his evil goals.

The very qualities we instill in our children; loving one another, respecting adults, being kind to all and obeying authority figures, are the "handles" that the molester, the pornographer and the deviate would use to destroy our children.

Because these godly teachings make our children particularly vulnerable to offenders, we must look to another principle in God's Word to provide the protection He would have us afford His little ones.

The answer to this difficult problem is touched upon in Hosea 4:6;

My people are destroyed for lack of knowledge: because thou hast rejected knowledge, I will also reject thee, that thou shalt be no priest to me: seeing thou has forgotten the law of thy God, I will also forget thy children. (Hosea 4:6) (KJV)

Part of your responsibility to God as a Christian parent is to teach your children the lessons that will help keep them safe; lessons that will give them the "knowledge" they lack.

It is with this conviction and an understanding of God's special plan for us and the children with which He has blessed us that this teaching is dedicated.

Used diligently, it will help equip you with an effective teaching tool for communicating the difficult realities of sexual assault to your children and will allow them to "walk uprightly in this crooked and perverse generation." (Philippians 2:15).

Notes

Actions, Often, Speak Louder Than Words!

Unfortunately, some children may not be able to tell you about their victim experiences without great difficulty.

Such children will, almost always, send out strong signals that the attentive and informed parent can use to alert him or her to the possibility of a problem.

The first thing you must do is begin to listen to the "funny" things that your child may say about any relationship he or she has with an adult.

These comments are especially important when they are out of context with the normal child/adult role.

Your child's comment about Mr. Brown's funny undershorts may mean only that she saw them on the clothesline in the neighbor's backyard. Or, this could be your child's way of telling you that your friend and neighbor, nice old Mr. Brown, has been doing things that your child is uncomfortable with and thinks you may not approve of.

Don't jump to conclusions . . . instead, listen to your child and ask him or her to explain.

You may only have to tell her the difference between daddy's boxer shorts and the jockey shorts other men prefer *or* you may have a victim child reaching out for help. The only way you will ever know is to let your child tell you.

Remember . . . a child who thinks no one is listening soon stops trying to tell you what is bothering him or her.

You should also be on the lookout for the child who exhibits seemingly irrational or unfounded fears of adults who were formerly favorites, or the child who does not wish to visit some family friend, or place of activity, which was formerly of great interest.

Look out for the child who may come to you with an unusual medical problem which can not be satisfactorily explained by the child (i.e., venereal disease, rectal bleeding, etc.).

Look out for the child who may become unusually interested in adultlike sexually oriented displays of affection or may express affection in a genitally oriented matter.

Some victimized children may have sudden sleep problems, others may not want to eat, or seem suddenly burdened with many new fears or need reassurance in things previously done independently. Some suddenly regress to more childlike behavior than normal.

If your child has been sexually assaulted, it is likely that the offender has suggested that, for various reasons, your child must keep the experience secret. This demand is often reinforced, in the child's mind, by guilt or confusion about the responsibility for the acts committed.

Remember, sexual assault is *always* a confusing and difficult experience for the victim, especially when the victim is a child.

All this puts great emotional stress on the child victim and often results in classic regressive behavior and acting out.

Again, not every behavioral change in your child's life will be attributable to this area of risk. However, all too often, children grow up carrying these secret scars and emotional trauma solely because their "signals" went unquestioned or were unfortunately misinterpreted.

Remember . . . . ACTIONS OFTEN SPEAK LOUDER THAN WORDS!

Know The Enemy!

Because child victim sexual assault is a subject which frightens and revolts most caring adults, it has become a topic of little real understanding and much confusion in our society at large, and to some greater extent in the Christian community.

To effectively deal with these potential dangers, it is helpful to understand some of the truths about this frightening and often avoided subject.

Your understanding of the sexual offender will be particularly helpful in responding to the questions children commonly ask during this teaching.

You must first understand that the person most likely to sexually assault your child is not the "dirty old man" that we all imagine.

It is most likely that the person who will sexually assault your child will be a respected, upstanding member of your community or neighborhood and someone who is already known to you or your child.

Sometimes the person who would involve your child in such immoral conduct will mask his evil with a falsely moral or religious lifestyle or high position in the community.

Most offenders can best be characterized as the "guy next door." They are almost always "average" and "normal" in their apparent lifestyle.

It is not unusual, when confronted with an accusation of sexual misconduct, for most offenders to strongly deny the allegations.

In cases where the offending person was actually caught in the act, or where the evidence is beyond any doubt, the typical child molester will most often plead sorrow, remorse, seek an excuse in drugs or alcohol or claim that he was seduced by the child.

No matter what the offender may say, we know, from experience, that these people are not likely to change their ways and will usually continue to repeat such vicious acts unless stopped by outside factors (either legal or institutional). However, even then, they are likely to offend again when released from supervision.

While most sexual assaults are committed by adult men, another group presents a real danger to your child and deserves your attention.

Surprisingly, that population is made up of adolescent boys. It may be difficult for you to believe that that nice teenager down the street could sexually assault your child, but on a statistical basis, more than 30% of the sexual assault cases in North America occur between teenaged boys and younger children of both sexes.

Such teenaged molesters are usually more identifiable from a behavioural model than their adult counterparts discussed above and therefore you should be aware of the following "Adolescent Offender Profile":

1. Male: 12-18 years old.
2. Does not relate well to children his own age.
3. Has few friends and can often be characterized as a "loner".
4. May have been sexually abused or the victim of physical abuse.
5. Tends to be subject to peer group rejection and seems isolated socially or at school.

6. Seeks out relationships and situations in which he is in a position of independent authority over younger children.

Please Note:

The Adolescent Offender Profile listed above is, by necessity, brief and inconclusive by itself. Not every person who exhibits some or all of these traits is a child molester and the absence of these traits is no guarantee of safety. It should be used as one of many factors that will assist you in your efforts to protect and educate your children.

Remember, your best protection is a secure, well-educated and informed child.

Notes

But What Do You Do If *It* Happens To Your Child?

If during your teaching you discover that your child has been sexually assaulted in the past; or, is presently being mishandled by someone; or, if your child reports an offense to you in the future, the following guidelines may help you.

It is most important that your initial reaction to such a discovery does not cause your child further trauma.

Be careful! Do not lose sight of the needs of your child. Now is the time for cool heads and loving hearts.

You should always keep in mind that it is almost unheard of for children to "make up" or fantasize acts of sexual assault. If your child can be specific enough to explain the physical aspects of a sexual assault, it is almost certain that he or she is telling you the tragic, but unembellished truth.

In that case, you can best help your child by restraining the natural tendency to prove the child wrong or to convince yourself that this is all a mistake on the child's part.

Most parents who have not been prepared for the experience instinctively attack or attempt to rebut the child's story in a misguided hope that, by doing so, they will resolve the issue as one of an untruthful child rather than that of a child victim.

PLEASE. . . DON'T MAKE THAT MISTAKE.

Instead, immediately tell your child the following things as calmly and supportively as you possibly can.

1. Tell your child that you believe he or she is telling you the truth and that what has happened is not, and was not, his or her fault;

2. Make it clear to your child that you are pleased that he or she has shared these facts with you and that you are *very* sorry that your child has been subjected to such an unhappy and hurtful experience; and

3. That you will do everything necessary to provide your child with all the help he or she needs to deal with this situation.

You should make it clear to your child that you are on his or her side and will advocate on the child's behalf throughout the events to come.

Remember, you may be overwhelmed by anger, guilt and helplessness all at once. *BUT IT'S YOUR CHILD WHO MUST BE HELPED FIRST.*

You are a parent and he or she is the child. This is the time to ask God for all the wisdom and strength He can provide.

Medical Care

If you discover that your child has been the victim of a sexual assault, the need for medical care becomes one thing that you, as a caring parent, must control.

In the event that the sexual assault has taken place within the last 18 to 24 hours, you should understand that in most cases, immediate emergency medical care will be required for your child.

Keep in mind that even if your child has escaped the assault without apparent physical injury, you should seek immediate medical help.

Because not all emergency medical facilities are created equal, now, not then, is the time to determine what medical facility in your community is prepared to deal with sexual assault cases in a manner that will best serve you and your child.

The way to do this is to call your local police department or emergency room facility and ask the questions:

1. Does our community have a rape crisis program?;

2. What special medical provision is made under such a program?; *and*

3. Does that program have a special child victim component?

Don't be too surprised if you find out that your community has no special program or, if it does have a program, that no specialized facility or personnel has been provided to deal with the child victim.

If that is the case, you must begin immediately to cause such a specialized service to be instituted in your community.

Do not accept answers like, "Any Emergency Room can handle the job," or "We just don't have that many child victim cases here in our nice town." They are untrue and inexcusable.

MAKE SURE YOUR COMMUNITY IS READY.

Your child might be the next person to need such help.

Once you determine that there is a properly staffed and equipped facility available to your child and following your discovery of your child's recent victimization you should do the following:

1. Do not change your child's clothes or bath or wash the child. This will be difficult, but you can best serve the needs of your child if you provide the necessary first aid to your child and take him or her *immediately* to an appropriate emergency medical facility.

2. Upon arrival at the medical facility, you should privately and quietly advise someone in authority of the reason for your visit and that you wish your child cared for.

You should also request that the police be notified of your child's examination and request that the medical staff cooperate with the police in the gathering of evidence.

DO NOT ASSUME THAT THIS IS AUTOMATIC if you have not yet spoken to the police, this is the time you should do so.

You should specifically request that the police initially limit their interrogation of your child to no more than one interview which should be conducted by a specially trained officer, preferably of the same sex as the child.

This is as good a time as any for such an interview to take place; however, keep in mind that you already know most of what the police need to know. While nearly everyone involved will want to hear the story, directly from your child, you will have to decide to whom and under what conditions these interrogations will take place.

Your child will not be helped if everyone from the first uniformed officers, to the sergeant, and the detectives and, then again, the sex crime specialist ask the same questions over and over, again and again.

It's your child — you must do what *you* think is best to protect him or her.

During the medical examination, the police should request that certain evidence be preserved, samples taken and the child's clothing retained as evidence.

That is a good sign that the police are taking the case seriously. It will, however, require that you bring a full change of clothing, including shoes and socks for your child to change into after the medical examination.

Another important part of your role in helping your child through this traumatic experience will be the ability to coordinate the various persons and agencies who have contact with your child.

Be prepared to *write things down*,
ask questions,
get answers and
write the answers down.

Get the names of the police, the doctors, nurses, the social workers and others you report to or who have examined your child.

Later you may want to, or need to, speak to one of these people. It is best to know their names and where to find them.

You will also be able to prevent some unnecessary, repetitious and often intrusive examinations and questioning of your child by being able to refer the police to the doctor, etc.

Most important of all, you should stay with your child no matter what anyone tells you. There are few times when a stranger can hold your child's hand or stroke his or her brow with greater effect than you can.

The best rule of thumb is to always remain with your child, give support and unless your child requires critical or surgical medical care, *tough it out.* Keep letting your child know that you are on his side, that things will be alright and that, to the extent possible, you will make sure your child's wishes are respected.

That's important

If things begin to center too much on other people's needs and not enough upon the needs of your child. *Slow them down.* That's what you are there for — BE THE PARENT GOD WANTS YOU TO BE!

Remember, you can not stop an uncaring doctor, nurse or policeman from further traumatizing your child if you are sitting in the waiting room biting your fingernails.

So, take a deep breath, and ask God for all the wisdom, guidance and strength you are going to need.

Believe me, the Lord will give you and your child the help you need to come through the ordeal.

Finally, if your child's personal family doctor has not been involved in, or notified of, the medical examination, have the hospital telephone, and then mail, a copy of the report to your child's doctor.

This is particularly important if the report indicates the need for further medical treatment for venereal disease or some other condition resulting from the assault.

Spiritual Care

The church, which is the body of Christ, is required to respond when any member of that body is hurt. There is, therefore, a spiritual responsibility of the church toward child victims and their families.

A child who has had the experience of sexual assault cannot be ignored — as if Christians were somehow immune.

They need understanding, prayerful support from family and friends, sound Biblical counselling, and the assurance that this life experience, like all experiences in life, can be overcome and transformed through Christ.

They can be greatly strengthened by continual reassurance of their value to, and position in, Christ.

> *Even when we are too weak to have any faith left, He remains faithful to us and will help us, for He cannot disown us who are part of Himself, and He will always carry out His promises to us." (2 Timothy 2:13)*

A direct corollary of this lesson is the realization that no matter what circumstances occur around or to the physical body, the position of the Christian in Christ is *never* in jeopardy — but rather "they shall never perish, neither shall any man pluck them out" of God's hand. (St. John 10:28).

This scriptural encouragement is not meant to imply that there is a simplistic or instant "Christian" solution to the devastation of sexual assault. The Christian does, however, have the spiritual resource of the Holy Spirit to carry him through such traumas, for, as Paul writes:

God never abandons us. We get knocked down, but we get up again and keep going." (2 Corinthians 4:9)

"We are pressed on every side by troubles, but not crushed and broken. We are perplexed because we don't know why things happen as they do, but we don't give up and quit." (2 Corinthians 4:8)

Your child may have been knocked down, but with the love of the Body of Christ, the support of you the parent and the infinite power of the Holy Spirit, your child will "get up again and keep going" firm in the knowledge that he or she is safe and loved.

Understanding Your Child's Activity Workbook

This section of your Teaching Guide is designed to familiarize you, on a page by page basis, with the Activity Workbook which your child will use during this Little Ones teaching.

It contains a complete reproduction of each teaching page of the Activity Workbook and individual teaching notes for the lessons your children will find before them.

It will be necessary for you to carefully review this section before beginning to lead your child through the study.

You must be familiar with each lesson before you attempt to teach it. This section will provide you with a complete understanding of the objectives, goals and options available to you in the course and will reveal the teaching aids that have been built into the Little Ones Activity Workbook.

You must also become familiar with the scriptural references on each page of the Activity Workbook. They will be of great significance in the teaching.

Notes

Lesson Number One

Pages 2-5

Teaching Objectives

This lesson is intended to provide your child with a basic understanding of the story of creation as is told in the Book of Genesis and the special place that people play in God's plan.

Pages 2 and 3

Begin this lesson by explaining the story of the creation of the heaven and earth and God's love for all of his creations.

Allow the child to connect the pattern of dots that make up God's hands as you tell the child the story of God's wonderful work.

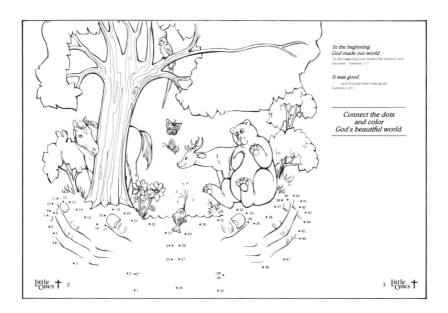

Page 4

This is the point at which you should introduce your child to the fact that God made people in His own image and that after He had done so, God confirmed that indeed, "it was very good!"

You should also take this opportunity to explain to your child God's plan for man on earth and His desire that we care for one another.

Then ask your child to draw a picture of someone caring for another person and ask him or her to tell you a story that the picture illustrates.

> ― *Then God made His most special creation — PEOPLE!* ―
> "Then God said, 'Let us make man in our image, in our likeness . . .'" (Genesis 1:26)
>
> *Do you know what God said when He created the first people? He said, "Very good!"*
> "God saw all that He had made and it was very good . . ." (Genesis 1:31)
>
> *People were made by God to care for His beautiful world . . .*
> "God blessed them and said to them, 'Be fruitful . . . fill the earth and subdue it. Rule over . . . every living creature . . .'" (Genesis 1:28)
>
> *and to care for each other.*
> ". . . love one another . . ." (John 13:34)
>
> *Draw a picture of someone caring for another.*
>
> Little Ones † 4

Page 5

Conclude this first lesson by teaching your child the beauty of giving thanks and praise to God for His love and His blessings.

At the close of this lesson, ask the child to draw and discuss the things that make him or her most thankful. Then point out to your child how God has provided these things as part of His creation.

Together . . .

People were to honor and love God with happy and thankful hearts for all the wonderful things He had done for them.

"It is good to praise the Lord." (Psalm 92:1)

What are some of the things YOU are thankful for? Can you draw them?

5 Little Ones †

Notes

Lesson Number Two

Pages 6 - 11

Teaching Objectives

This lesson is intended to reinforce the child's personal understanding of his or her place in a God created world; and to show your child how God has given us a unique ability of self-determination and the senses to help us in properly using that self-determination.

Page 6

Do you know that YOU are a special person?
"How precious it is, Lord, to realize that you are thinking about me constantly!" (Psalm 139:17a) (TLB)

God formed you in secret inside your mother's body.
"You made all the delicate, inner parts of my body and knit them together in my mother's womb." (Psalm 139:13) (TLB)

Do you know what God said when He made YOU? He said, "Very good!"

Draw a picture of yourself!

Little Ones † 6

Parents Teaching Guide

Begin this lesson by reviewing how God created mankind in His own image. Then follow the key text and scriptural references to reinforce the child's understanding of God's continued control over the creation of life. Particularly relate God's involvement in the things that led to *your* child's birth.

Have your child draw a picture of himself or herself.

This is a good time to discuss, with your child, the love God has for all His children, how both you and your child are "God's children", and how happy you are that God blessed you both with each other.

Page 7

When God made you, He gave you many wonderful parts.
"I praise you because I am fearfully and wonderfully made; your works are wonderful . . ." (Psalm 139:14)

The INSIDE of you has a "thinker" . . .
            a "feeler" . . .
            and a "chooser".

Your THINKER helps you learn new things.

Talk about some of the things you like to THINK about!
". . . whatever is true . . . noble . . . right . . . pure . . . lovely . . . admirable - if anything is excellent or praiseworthy - think about such things." (Philippians 4:8)

Aren't you glad God gave you a thinker?

7 Little Ones †

This page addresses the issue of God's gift of thought.

At this point you should explain to your child that God has provided each of us with a "thinker", a "feeler" and a "chooser".

Explain to your child how God would like him or her to use their "thinkers".

Discuss how we can all use our "thinker" to fulfill God's plan.

Pages 8 and 9

This page deals with the child's understanding of how his feelings fit into God's plan of self-determination.

Discuss all the feelings shown and follow the key texts on these pages to assist you in understanding your child's scope of feelings.

Our "feeler" is another one of our inside parts.

Here are some of the FEELINGS we sometimes have:

Color the faces of the feelings you have felt.

Talk about some other feelings you have had.

Which feelings make you feel good?

Which ones don't?

Happy

Scared

Mad

Loved

Mixed-up

Sad

little Ones ✝ 8

9 little Ones ✝

Page 10 and 11

At this point, you must explain to the child how God has given us the ability to *think* and *feel* so that we may *choose*.

Concentrate on how the ability to make free will choice is truly, God's most special gift of all three.

Follow the key texts on page 11 and conclude with a discussion of the types of free will choices that you and your child have made that day.

You may want to use the illustration and prayer on page 10 as an example of a free will choice that everyone has the ability to make.

Lesson Number Three

Pages 12 - 15

Teaching Objectives

This lesson introduces the child to the human body. It is intended to provide the child with an understanding of the difference between those parts of his or her body which are "public" and those which are "private". In addition, it provides an opportunity to distinguish the difference between the male and female body.

If your child lacks a detailed understanding of his or her own body, this is the time for you to make sure that this information is imparted.

If your child is unfamiliar with the body parts of the opposite sex, you should make sure that you explain the basic differences between boys (men) and girls (women).

Don't be embarrassed to discuss this subject candidly with your child. You are only giving your child the "knowledge" that he or she needs about the body that God has created for us to dwell in.

Pages 12 and 13

Discuss, with your child, the body parts which are illustrated on these pages. Ask your child to identify these body parts and discuss their usefulness and how wonderful their use is. Talk about how good it is that God gave you both such useful and well thought-out parts.

Discuss the differences between the parts that are usually open to view and those which are not.

Allow your child to ask lots of questions.

Follow the teaching keys and take the time to be sure that your child has resolved *all* questions he or she may have regarding his or her genitalia.

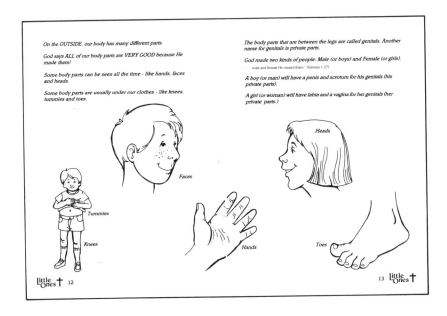

On the OUTSIDE, our body has many different parts.

God says ALL of our body parts are VERY GOOD because He made them!

Some body parts can be seen all the time - like hands, faces and heads.

Some body parts are usually under our clothes - like knees, tummies and toes.

The body parts that are between the legs are called genitals. Another name for genitals is private parts.

God made two kinds of people: Male (or boys) and Female (or girls).
" ... male and female He created them." (Genesis 1:27)

A boy (or man) will have a penis and scrotum for his genitals (his private parts).

A girl (or woman) will have labia and a vagina for her genitals (her private parts.)

Heads

Faces

Tummies

Knees

Hands

Toes

Little Ones † 12

13 Little Ones †

It may be helpful to relate this teaching to the child's personal knowledge of his brothers, sisters or other relatives or acquaintances.

This is an important lesson and you should take all the time needed for your child to understand it.

Pages 14 and 15

At this point, you should ask the child to identify what sex he or she is and to describe the parts of the body.

You should also take this opportunity to make sure that your child understands that God made our bodies, that He made us in His image and that whatever we do to our body, we are doing to a part of God's creation.

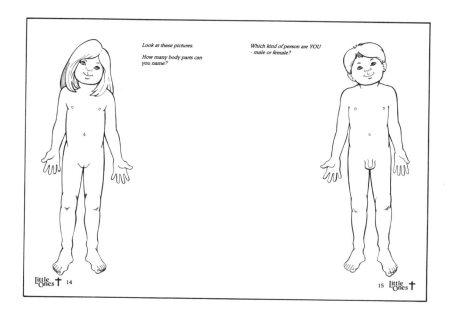

Look at these pictures.

How many body parts can you name?

Which kind of person are YOU - male or female?

Now is the time to be sure that the child understands the positive nature of his or her body and the responsibility to use it for the fulfillment of God's plan.

Author's Note:

If you think that your child requires additional study material in the area of instruction covered by this lesson, we would suggest that you obtain a copy of "You're Either One Or The Other" by Joy Wilt, published by Word, Incorporated of Waco, Texas.

Notes

Lesson Number Four

Pages 16 - 17

Teaching Objectives

This lesson is intended to lead the child through the five senses and concludes in a discussion of the sense of TOUCH.

Pages 16-17

Follow the teaching keys and discuss how our senses are God given, are wonderful and all very useful in our everyday life.

Ask your child to answer the questions which make up the teaching keys and have him or her explain their favorite sensory experiences.

Besides giving us our inside and outside parts, God gave us even more gifts!

Every good and perfect gift is from above, coming down from the Father (James 1.17)

These gifts are called our SENSES.

Ears that hear and eyes that see . . . the Lord has made them both. (Proverbs 20.12)

They help us to understand what is going on around us.

They make our life very interesting.

We have five of them:

Hearing

Seeing

Tasting

Touching

Smelling

What is your favorite thing to SEE?

What sound do you like to HEAR?
Can you make the sound?

What TASTES good to you?
Tell why you like it.

What do you like to SMELL?
Can a smell make you feel happy?

What is something you like to TOUCH?
What does it feel like?

Our senses help us enjoy God's world and God's people.

We are going to use the rest of the book to learn some things about . . . our sense of TOUCH.

Little Ones † 16

17 Little Ones †

Notes

Lesson Number Five

Pages 18 - 23

Teaching Objectives

This lesson is intended to convey, to your child, the scope and positive nature of appropriate touching.

We will use the term "YES TOUCH" to identify such appropriate touching.

Pages 18 and 19

Discuss with your child how much you both like to be touched and hugged and how good it feels. Take a moment to show your child what kind of touch you enjoy and how you like to hug him or her.

Ask your child to share his or her feeling about such "YES TOUCHES."

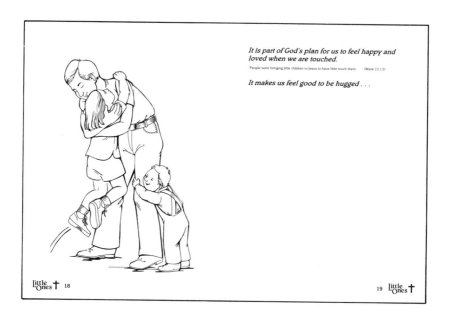

It is part of God's plan for us to feel happy and loved when we are touched.

"People were bringing little children to Jesus to have Him touch them   (Mark 10:13)

It makes us feel good to be hugged . . .

little Ones † 18

19 little Ones †

Parents Teaching Guide

Take a minute and share a "YES TOUCH" or two with your child. Share with your child how much joy you get when he or she hugs you and how hugs like the ones that you and your child share are good and part of God's plan for the proper use of the body He gave us.

Pages 20 and 21

to hold hands with a friend . . .

or to snuggle up with someone we love . . .

Use these illustrations to assist you in your dialogue of "YES TOUCHES."

Ask your child to tell you a story about each illustration.

This is also the point in the teaching that you should introduce your child to a symbol which is used to indicate "YES TOUCHES" throughout the workbook.

This symbol, which appears at the bottom of pages 20 and 21, as well as elsewhere in the workbook, represents the praising child.

We have chosen this symbol to represent the thankful attitude that we should all exhibit to God for His blessings.

It is up to you to choose the degree to which you emphasize this symbol and its scriptural and social significance.

Pages 22 and 23

This is the point at which your child should understand the term "YES TOUCH" as the positive and appropriate use of touch.

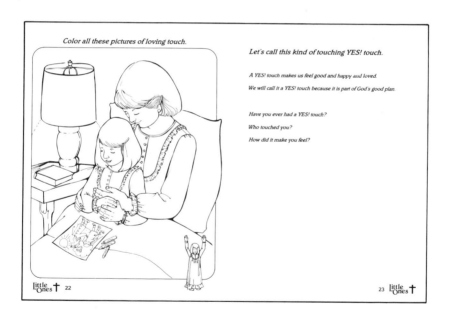

Color all these pictures of loving touch.

Let's call this kind of touching YES! touch.

A YES! touch makes us feel good and happy and loved.
We will call it a YES! touch because it is part of God's good plan.

Have you ever had a YES! touch?
Who touched you?
How did it make you feel?

Follow the questions contained in the teaching keys to be sure that your child understands what a "YES TOUCH" is.

Notes

Lesson Number Six

Pages 24 - 31

Teaching Objectives

This is the lesson in which you are going to teach your child about what we will be calling "NO TOUCH."

You will be teaching your child the difference between good and evil and the free will use of God's gifts.

This is the longest and most significant lesson in the course and should not be rushed.

You may wish to break this lesson into two sessions separated by a brief period that will allow you and the child to question each other outside the formal teaching setting.

If you choose to do so, we recommend that you begin the second session of this lesson with a review of the first.

Pages 24 and 25

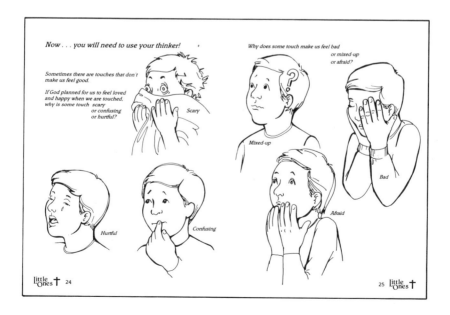

Follow the teaching keys and discuss each point with your child.

Use the illustrations to lead your child into a dialogue of his or her own feelings.

Pages 26 and 27

It is very important that you take time, at this point, to reinforce the role that God plays in our life and to reaffirm God's loving involvement in each and every aspect of our creation and the obligations which are involved in our relationship with God.

Explain to your child how God gave every person on earth the ability to choose or self-determine.

Explain that God does not make us do things against our will . . . even if they are things we should do, according to His law.

Tell your child that, even when our wilful disobedience causes God to be unhappy with our sins, He never takes away our power to choose and always continues to love us.

Let's remember that when God made people, they were to love and obey Him.

Let's remember that God loved people so much He gave them a chooser.

That way, people could CHOOSE to obey God because they loved Him.

But . . .

because people have a chooser, they can choose NOT to love or obey God.

They can choose to HURT God by hurting some of the other people God made.

They can choose to use God's good body parts in bad ways.

Therefore, God gave them over to the sinful desires of their hearts to sexual impurity for the degrading of their bodies with one another. (Romans 1:24)

They can choose to use God's good gift of touch to hurt or scare others.

That is why some touch is scary, confusing or hurtful.

That is why some touch makes us feel bad or mixed-up or afraid.

little Ones † 26

27 little Ones †

Pages 28 and 29

This is the point at which you will introduce the child to the "NO TOUCH" symbol (page 28).

This symbol is intended to convey, to your child, the idea that his or her right to choose includes the God given power to choose to resist a "NO TOUCH".

This is particularly important within the context of the obedient personalties with which we strive to equip our children.

Your child must understand, at this point in the teaching, that he or she has a God given right to say NO to a "NO TOUCH" *because* a "NO TOUCH" is *NEVER PART OF GOD'S PLAN*.

Discuss with your child, using the illustration on page 29, the fact that he or she can not tell a "NO TOUCH" person just by the way they look. Follow the teaching keys to help the child understand this point.

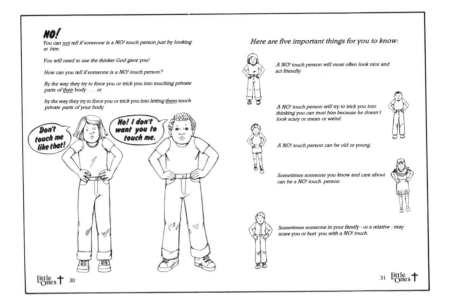

This is the conclusion of the lesson on "NO TOUCH".

Take the time to follow each teaching key and to make sure that your child understands each point before you go on to the next.

Discuss, with your child, the way the children in the illustrations on these pages are resisting the "NO TOUCHES" described in the teaching.

Ask your child to tell you what these boys and girls are thinking and saying.

This is the point at which you should know if your child understands what a "YES TOUCH" is and what a "NO TOUCH" is.

He or she should now understand that we praise God for the blessings of our "YES TOUCHES" and that we have God given authority to resist each and every "NO TOUCH" or "NO TOUCH PERSON" that Satan may confront us with.

Lesson Number Seven

Pages 32 - 51

Teaching Objectives

This lesson consists of a series of individual risk situations which your child will face in the world.

Each situation allows for significant input and personalization on your part.

Feel free to interject the important personal and community standards that fit into the situations illustrated in this lesson.

Pages 32 and 33

Review the previous teachings with your child using the teaching keys on page 33.

Again, if you sense any misunderstanding of the teaching, now is a good time to go back and review.

Feel free to repeat any or all of the workbook before continuing.

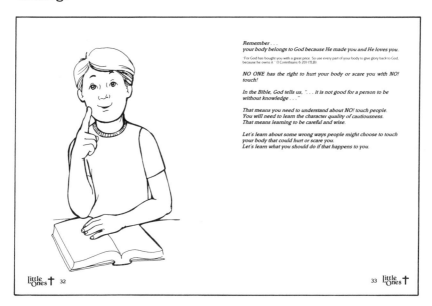

Remember . . .
your body belongs to God because He made you and He loves you.

"For God has bought you with a great price. So use every part of your body to give glory back to God, because he owns it." (I Corinthians 6:20) (TLB)

NO ONE has the right to hurt your body or scare you with NO! touch!

In the Bible, God tells us, ". . . it is not good for a person to be without knowledge . . ."

That means you need to understand about NO! touch people. You will need to learn the character quality of cautiousness. That means learning to be careful and wise.

Let's learn about some wrong ways people might choose to touch your body that could hurt or scare you. Let's learn what you should do if that happens to you.

Little Ones † 32

33 Little Ones †

Little Ones † 34

If a person is following you or wants to know your name and where your house is he might be a NO! touch person. You do not have to tell anyone where you live or what your name is. Run to your house or wherever you know there will be someone at home. Tell your dad or mom right away about that person.

Let's pretend you are walking home from school. A big boy starts to walk behind you. He acts friendly and tells you he just moved into a house by your house. He asks you your name and which house you live in. What should you do?

USE YOUR THINKER!

Is it a lie if you don't tell him your name or where you live?

Where would you run to? Who would you tell?

What if you knew no one was home at your house?

35 little
Ones †

Little Ones † 36

If someone comes to your house when no one else is home and asks you to let him come in to use the phone - or for any other reason - he might be a NO! touch person. Do not open the door or let him come in no matter how nice he looks. Be sure to tell your dad or mom about that person just as soon as they get home.

Let's pretend you are watching TV and dad is at work. Mom just went to the store for some milk and will be gone a few minutes. You are home by yourself. The doorbell rings and a handsome man is standing there. He is wet from standing in the rain and he looks like he needs help. What should you do?

USE YOUR THINKER!

Should you unlock the door just to ask what he wants?

Should you let him use the phone?

Should you try to help him, or should you let a grownup at some other house help him?

Is it unkind if you do not unlock the door and help him?

Or - is it wise if you do not unlock the door?

37 Little Ones †

If a person is showing you his genitals (his private parts) he is a NO! touch person. You should run away from that person and tell your dad or mom right away.

Let's pretend you are at the park. You recognize a man from your neighborhood. He is passing out candy to other children. You go over to him and then see that the man has his pants unzipped and he is exposing his private parts to you. What should you do?

USE YOUR THINKER!

Should you run away?

Who could you tell?

Did you do anything wrong?

Did that man do anything wrong? Why?

39 little Ones †

If someone asks you for directions, that is OK. But if that person tries to get you to come into their car or tries to take you away, he is a NO! touch person. You should run and find a grown-up right away. Run away from the direction the car is going. Tell your dad or mom right away what that person wanted you to do.

Let's pretend you are pulling your wagon on the sidewalk. A car slows down and stops beside you. It is a pretty car and the man inside is wearing a nice suit. He tells you he is looking for a certain ice cream store. He asks you to get in the car to show him where the store is. He says he will buy you an ice cream cone to thank you for going with him. What should you do?

USE YOUR THINKER!

Would you get in the car?

Would you talk any more to that person?

Where would you run?

Who could you tell right away?

Would you worry about leaving your wagon on the sidewalk?

41 little Ones †

Little Ones † 42

If a person who knows your family or a relative touches your private parts, or tries to force or trick you into touching their private parts, that is a NO! touch.

If someone you know makes you do things you do not understand, or touches you and tells you to keep it a secret, that is NO! touch.

ALWAYS tell someone you trust about ANY touch that is confusing to you! You can tell dad, mom, a teacher, a policeman, or a grown-up friend.

This is a story about Suzie. She is 9. Suzie was visiting her aunt and uncle. Everyone was busy in the kitchen and Suzie and her uncle were watching TV. Her uncle was tickling her and then began to feel under her clothes. He had done this before and always told Suzie to keep it a secret. Suzie did not like this kind of touch. What do you think Suzie should do?

Was this a NO! touch? Did Suzie do anything wrong?

Did the uncle do anything wrong?

Would it be hard for Suzie to tell her dad or mom about what her uncle did?

Should Suzie obey her uncle and keep this touching a secret - or -

should Suzie obey her parents who had taught her to always tell them if someone touched her in a way she didn't like?

If any person wants you to go alone in an alley or in the bushes or in an empty room with him, he is a NO! touch person. RUN! Tell your dad or mom or another grown-up right away. A policeman is a good person to tell.

Let's pretend a nice young man smiles at you and tells you he has some kitties in a basket in the alley behind his house. He says you can hold one and even take one home if you'd like to. What should you do?

USE YOUR THINKER!

Should you go into the alley to look at the kitties just for a minute?

Should you stay and talk to that person and ask him more about the kitties?

Should you run away and not talk to that person any more?

Who would you tell what that person wanted you to do?

Is it important enough for you to interrupt dad or mom to tell them about it right away?

45 little Ones †

Little Ones † 46

Let's pretend you are taking a walk. You see an older man carrying a bag of groceries. He is walking slow. He stops to tell you how heavy his bag is and how hard it is for him to carry it. He asks if you would carry it for him to his back door. Mom and Dad have taught you to be kind and helpful and this old man looks like he needs help. What should you do?

USE YOUR THINKER!

Should you carry his groceries for him without first asking permission from your parents?

Is it unkind if you don't help him?

Is it wise for you to run to your dad or mom and tell what this person asked you to do?

47 Little Ones †

Little Ones † 48

If someone calls your house on the telephone and says bad words that scare you - or if someone just breathes funny in the phone when you answer - that is called an obscene phone call. You should HANG UP the phone right away! Then go and tell your dad or mom what happened.

Let's pretend you are helping mom in the kitchen. The phone rings and mom is too busy to answer it. You are helpful and answer it for her. The person who is calling says words on the phone that you don't understand and then makes funny breathing noises. What should you do?

USE YOUR THINKER!

Should you tell that person he is naughty to say those things?

Should you ask your mommy to talk to him?

Should you hang up right away?

Should you tell your dad or mom right after the call?

49 Little Ones †

This is a story about Mike. He is 4 years old. Mike has a cousin who is 14 and babysits him a lot. Mike likes his cousin and they have lots of fun together. Sometimes Mike's cousin makes Mike play a game that Mike doesn't understand. Mike's cousin makes Mike touch him between his legs. Mike does not like to touch his cousin like that. His cousin makes Mike promise not to tell. Mike is afraid to tell. What should Mike do?

USE YOUR THINKER!

Did Mike do anything wrong?

Did Mike's cousin do anything wrong?

Should Mike tell someone about this NO! touch?

Who do you think he should tell?

51 Little Ones †

Notes

Lesson Number Eight

Page 52

Teaching Objectives

This is the conclusion of the Little Ones course.

You should take this opportunity to celebrate the meaningful lessons that you and your child have shared.

Use these pages to review the teaching and reinforce your child's understanding of God's plan for him and his personal relationship with the Lord.

You have been using your thinker a lot. We have learned a lot of new things.

Now let's use your "feeler".

You can feel GLAD to know that almost all touches are YES! touches!

You can feel HAPPY to know that God loves you!

"We know how much God loves us because we have felt His love and because we believe Him when He tells us that He loves us dearly." (I John 5:16a) (TLB)

You can feel THANKFUL to know that your dad or mom loves you so much that they would read this book with you!

"He who fears the Lord has a secure fortress, and for his children it will be a refuge." (Proverbs 14:26)

You can feel PROUD to know that you are growing up and becoming wise!

"Listen, my son, to your father's instruction and do not forsake your mother's teaching." (Proverbs 1:8)

---

*You can feel SPECIAL
because you are loved so much!*

Notes